TO JEAN AND JOE

TRUE
EAST

[signature]

August, 2006

CREDITS

PUBLISHED BY

Peconic Land Trust
296 Hampton Road, PO Box 1776
Southampton, New York 11969
1.631.283.3195
www.peconiclandtrust.org

Copyright © 2006 Wendy Chamberlin, Bridgehampton, New York
No part of the contents of this book may be reproduced by any
electronic or mechanical means without the written permission
of the publishers.

Foreword copyright © 2006 John v.H. Halsey, President,
Peconic Land Trust

May 2006

ISBN# 0-615-13139-5

COLOPHON

Author/Photography: Wendy Chamberlin,
Bridgehampton, New York

Editor: Michael Shnayerson, Bridgehampton, New York

Design: Steven Mosier, New York • Texas

Print Production: Working Dog Press, Whately, Massachusetts

Image Seperations: Gist and Herlin, West Haven, Connecticut

Printing: C&C Offset Printing Co., Ltd., Shenzhen, China

Printed and bound in China

CONTENTS

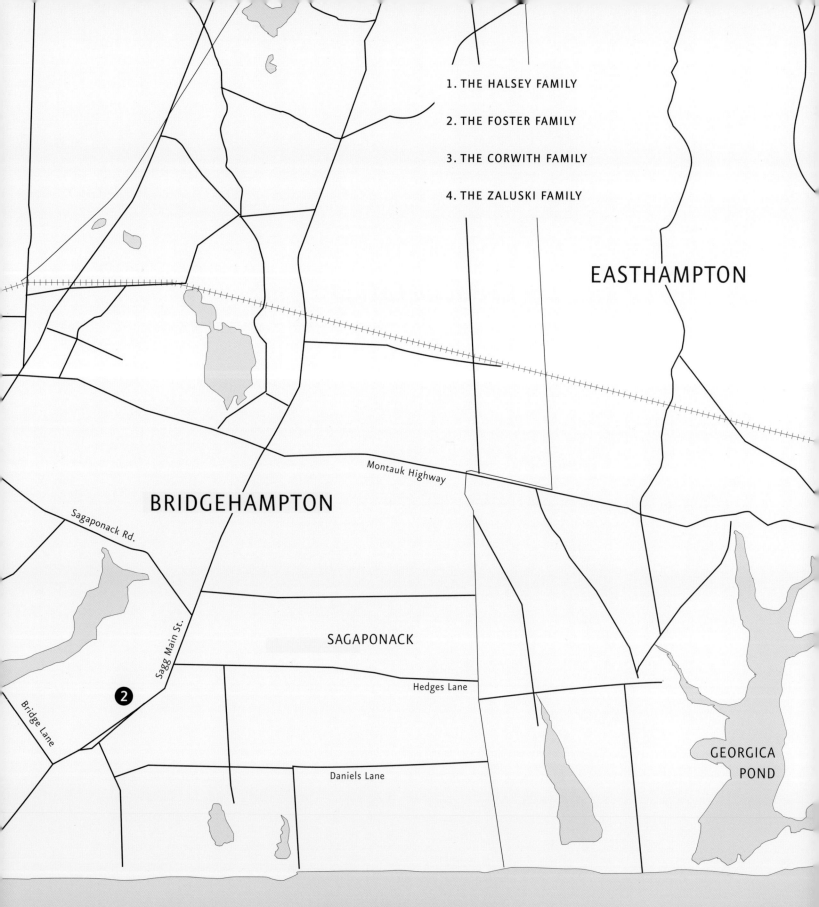

1. THE HALSEY FAMILY

2. THE FOSTER FAMILY

3. THE CORWITH FAMILY

4. THE ZALUSKI FAMILY

EASTHAMPTON

Montauk Highway

BRIDGEHAMPTON

Sagaponack Rd.

SAGAPONACK

Sagg Main St.

Hedges Lane

Bridge Lane

❷

Daniels Lane

GEORGICA
POND

ATLANTIC OCEAN

FOREWORD

By documenting the lives of four farm families on Eastern Long Island, True East reveals that farming is not simply a livelihood, it is a way of life that is not only rich in history, but also one that is in jeopardy.

I have had the good fortune of spending most of my life on the "East End," as have 11 generations of my branch of the Halsey family before me. During my high school years in the late 1960's, I worked on one of many Halsey farms where I quickly learned to become a jack of all trades. When I was not working in the fields or carrying irrigation pipes across rows of potatoes, I was shingling a water tower or painting equipment in a barn. Everyday was an adventure and every hour was put to good use. I came to appreciate not only the multitude of skills and activities that I was exposed to on the farm, but also the independence and ingenuity of farmers.

After college, I lived in other parts of the world for 10 years, returning to visit my family and friends during the summer months. On my visit in 1980, I was shocked and dismayed to see "For Sale" signs on the farm next door. This farm had been in the same family for 10 generations. Just outside the back door of the farmstead, there were 250 acres of rich Bridgehampton loam less than 1/4 mile from the Atlantic Ocean. I called the family and learned that their parents had passed away and that there was a $2.2 million estate tax due. Not having that kind of money in the bank, the family had to sell the farm to a developer in order to pay the tax.

This unfortunate situation brought about the founding of the Peconic Land Trust. In 1983, along with a local farmer, a town planning board member, and a teacher, I incorporated the Trust, a nonprofit, tax-exempt organization dedicated to conserving Long Island's working farms, natural lands, and heritage for our communities now and in the future. Since then, a team of professional staff, volunteer Board members, contributors, public agencies, and landowners has worked to protect thousands of acres of fertile soils and natural resources. Today, the obstacles facing the continuation of agriculture on the East End of Long Island are staggering. Federal estate tax policy, high land values, zoning and pesticide regulations, loss of farmer equity, and complaints from new neighbors represent just a few of the issues challenging the very existence of family farms here and across the country.

If family farms are to survive on the East End of Long Island, together with the rich heritage that they represent, the public at large must understand that protecting the business of farming is as critical as protecting the farmland itself. Efforts to conserve working farms must be based upon understanding and respecting the needs, goals, and circumstances of farm families as well as the opportunities and dilemmas associated with their land. True East presents an invaluable perspective that will enable the public to better understand family farms and the special connection that they have to the land. Their stewardship of important soil resources, not to mention the fruits (and vegetables) of their labor, are an inspiration. With a greater appreciation of all that farming entails and the challenges that it faces, there is a real opportunity to further mobilize our communities to support the working farms that define our agricultural heritage and provide an invaluable local food source today and for the future.

John v.H. Halsey, President
The Peconic Land Trust

INTRODUCTION

This slender strip of golden soil, known as the South Fork of Long Island, is the work of two million years of glaciers. Lying between graceful bays to the north and the majestic Atlantic Ocean to the south, it has seven small villages along one highway, settled in order from west to east, beginning in 1640, from Southampton to Montauk. Just fifty years ago, the villages were small clusters surrounded on all sides by open fields, framed by woods, sky and water. Today each town is larger, with thickets of outlying houses. And yet farm fields remain. Tractors still plow and plant the soil – with vegetables, fruits and flowers – as if in a race with the bull-dozers that scrape the fields beside them to make way for new houses. Weekenders, even long-time locals, cast a glance as they drive by at the weathered barns and silos of those working farms, the tilled furrows flanked by burgeoning McMansions, and assume the farmers are a dying breed. Not true. In spite of the many challenges these farm families face, agriculture in Suffolk County generates more revenue than any other county of New York State: $200 million. Many of these remaining farms belong to families who have successfully husbanded the same land for generations. Three of the four families represented in this book trace their Long Island farming forebears to the mid-17th century. The fourth family belongs to a later generation from Poland. Like their English and Irish predecessors, they came to Long Island to exercise the right of self determination and found a temperate garden, bountiful beyond their wildest immigrants' dreams.

The soil that gave those families opportunity in the new world owes much of its existence to the Wisconsin ice sheet. This last of the Pleistocene epoch glaciers, two miles thick in places and two thousand feet high at its leading edge, advanced over the South Fork at a rate of about 400 feet a year, pushing rocks and sediment in front of it like an enormous snowplow. As the climate began intermittently to warm, previous glaciers had retreated, advanced, and retreated again, pulverizing their loads into a perfect mixture of silt, clay and sand, unique to this area and designated by the U.S. Department of Agriculture as "Bridgehampton Loam." When the Wisconsin glacier finally retreated, as much as two feet of Bridgehampton loam was spread over fifty square miles between Southampton and Amagansett.

The Algonquin people, of course, discovered this perfect soil long before European settlers. Arriving 12,500 years ago as nomadic hunters, they developed techniques for cultivating maize, tobacco, squash, beans, melons, pumpkins and gourds. The South Fork is ideal for agriculture due to the fact that the Gulf Stream comes closer to Long Island than any other part of the east coast, moderating the climate and providing the Northeast's longest growing period: 220 days.

To the Algonquins, Long Island was Paumanok, for "fish-shaped," and Southampton was Agawam, so called for the abundance of shells found there. Two kinds of shells were manufactured by the Indians into wampum, which by 1628 became the legal tender of the Europeans as well. Giovanni Verrazano, the first European to sail along the south shore of Long Island in 1524, wrote in his journal that he saw many fires along the coast at night. The Algonquins befriended the Europeans who came, but for their hospitality they incurred small pox, typhus, influenza and measles; at least as many succumbed to alcohol, for which they had no physiological tolerance. By 1658, as few as 500 remained on the East End. Today they have rebounded. The Halsey, Foster and Corwith families were there to witness that sad diminution. All three had emigrated to America from England by the late 1630's.

The lives that Thomas Halsey, Christopher Foster and Digory Corwith had enjoyed in England were privileged compared to most of their countrymen. They were landowners, from Bedfordshire, Surrey and Cornwall, and all belonged to the rank of yeomen, a step above husbandman. But the kingdom of Charles I was plagued by military misadventures and corruption, and the Anglican church was purging Puritans. Fleeing widespread domestic disorder, thousands braved the Atlantic crossing in cramped and germ-ridden ships. The survivors, including Halseys, Fosters and Corwiths, landed weeks or even months later in Massachusetts.

Unfortunately, after settling in Lynn, Thomas Halsey and Christopher Foster soon found Puritan New England as restrictive as the mother country. On March 10th of 1639, Thomas joined in with a small group of settlers to buy a small boat for 80 pounds and passage to new, reportedly fertile lands on Long Island. In a document drawn up and signed by all, each man was consigned a house lot, planting lot and farm. They also outlined the first semblance of a zoning code in Southampton, clearly stating their desire to prevent overbuilding, overcrowding and to preserve farmland. "Only one dwelling house shall be built on each house lot and planting lots shall never be made house lots, whereby more inhabitants might be received into the plantation causing the overcharging and impoverishment of all in the town." Christopher left Lynn to settle first in Hempstead, then he joined the settlement in Southampton.

The South Fork these hardy settlers saw when they sailed into its bays was as abundant in flora and fauna as the settlers' vision of the Garden of Eden. The Dutch had settlements primarily on western Long Island. Lion Gardiner was the only white man living this far out on the Island he claimed for his own.

From their landing at North Sea Harbor, the first settlers and their families walked down an old trail through meadows and forests that today is North Sea Road. Wildflowers were blooming in profusion. Wild fowl alighted on the branches and darted through underbrush. Huge flocks of migratory birds had returned from the south. The meadow lark, oriole, tanager, thrush, warbler, bobolink, wren, hummingbird and others filled the woods, meadows and the air itself with their songs. The settlers could reach out and grab handfuls of huckleberries, raspberries and strawberries, all in spring abundance, painting the woods and fields a brilliant red.

The settlers traveled south to a spot of elevated land by a stream that ran into a pond by the ocean. At these fertile acres, their voyage ended. This first settlement, later called "Olde Towne," lay in the same area where Southampton Hospital now stands. Everything was at hand: trees for house-building and firewood, game, fish, seaweed for manuring, and insulation for their homes, meadow grass for wintering livestock, and the soil itself for crops. By 1648 the settlement had spilled over to what is now Southampton's Main Street. Houses were probably built in the saltbox style, two stories in front with a slanting rear roof , the front facing south, no matter how the road ran, to take advantage of the sun and "purging breezes." These first farmers of the South Fork were resourceful and tireless because they had no choice: all they ate, bartered with and wore had to be raised on their farms. For trade in the city and closer at home, they produced the currency of the region; beef, pork, wheat, rye and whale oil, from whales they caught or washed up on the beaches. The most skilled among them built sloops or two-masted schooners for travel and trade along the ocean coast or the Sound to New Amsterdam. By ship they could take wood, hay and grain to sell or trade. During winter months when the migration of whales shifted to southern waters, it was not uncommon for men in whale boats to travel to New Jersey and Maryland, staying in makeshift shacks on the beaches to wait for their prey. Sheep, goats and cattle grazed on Shinnecock Hills – now site of the well-known golf course – and also out at Montauk Point. Buffalo could still be found on the east coast at that time and there are reports that they were used to pull a plow or cart.

A matter of considerable concern to the town's inhabitants was the wandering of each other's beasts and the damage done thereby. Many regulations were devised to keep beasts properly fenced. "Little piggs" required a special addendum to the general laws due to their inherent ability to walk under a regulation fence. Many disputes arose over whose cow broke a neighbor's fence, and who was liable for repairs. Often an owner chose simply not to claim the offending beast, and so there was a special fenced-in meadow called "the pound" allocated for these orphaned trespassers.

By the end of the 1600's the struggle for existence in a new land was coming to an end. The villages of the settlers had increased in size. Trade was in progress up and down both shores and contact with the outer world was greatly increased. Because of this, it was no longer imperative that each man be a jack-of-all-trades and people began to specialize into separate trades. The predominant of these was farming.

Freed from other tasks to focus entirely on how to increase the yield from his fields, the South Fork farmer soon employed gristmills driven by wind, tide and small streams to do much of his work and enable him to grow larger crops. Soon Long Island was one of the most important producing regions of the North American coast. Wheat from Long Island flowed into New York City and shipped to the sugar-producing islands of the West Indies. The potato was a latecomer. Having been brought back to Europe from South America by the Spanish, it was not introduced to North America as a domestic crop until 1719, when Scotch-Irish immigrants first planted potatoes in New Hampshire.

When the whaling industry boomed in the mid-18th century, farmers sold their crops to ships. By the 1870's the whaling industry had died out due to over fishing and the discovery of petroleum in Pennsylvania. The railroad arrived in the nick of time, reaching Southampton in 1870. Now crops traveled in hours, not days, to New York City. On the return trips, the trains brought manure from New York stables to fertilize the fields, and then commercial seeds and fertilizers. In the l890s, New Yorkers began building summer houses by the shore, in Southampton as well as East Hampton, and the farmers sold to them, too.

The South Fork farmers discovered potatoes soon after the turn with the century. Large open fields took over the landscape. Bigger fields meant more mechanization, first carried out with horse-drawn plows. The first tractors were made in approximately 1892 but Adam Halsey believes the first tractors out on the Island were probably Henry Ford's Fordsons, circa 1917. The first potato harvester was made in the 1920's, and was pulled by horses. It dug the potatoes up and left them on the surface to be picked up by hand. Mechanized harvesters arrived in the 1950s, ending the desultory work of past potato harvests. By then, potatoes were the main crop on the East End.

For a while, Long Island was potatoes. In 1969, it was the country's sixth-largest market in potato production. By 1997, it ranked 49th. The cause was obvious to all: beginning in the 1960s, the South Fork was valuable real estate. One acre of land brought $5,000 on the market. Potatoes on that acre would yield just $700 a year. Many farmers sold their land. Land values continued to rise and were reflected in inheritance taxes: heirs were forced to sell their families farms. The growing influx of second-home owners from the city also made moving the large equipment needed for planting and harvesting much more difficult. In 1965 Tom Halsey remembers owning 100 acres but farming 250 by leasing land from other farmers. Today those acres have houses on them. His son Adam remembers hearing his father say, as he surveyed a nearby farm field, "I used to farm that land." Today, at only twenty-three, Adam is already saying the same words.

Today the only large undeveloped areas left on Long Island are in Suffolk County, where the South Fork lies, and most of those acres are farmland. Ten years ago the county had 28,100 acres of land under cultivation. Today that number has fallen to approximately 26,000 acres. America's agricultural heritage is vanishing, nowhere more quickly than on Long Island's East End. Yet in our midst live guardians of this heritage whose ancestors planted the first seeds of our new world culture, almost 400 years ago. In their work and community, their forebears lived the tenets of Jeffersonian democracy. To a heartening degree, their descendents still practice those values. Through photographs and words, True East is a record of these family farms and the landscapes they nurture.

THE HALSEY FAMILY

Mary Halsey, Charles' wife and her aunt Susan Abigail Halsey Sweezy,
circa 1915, Halsey Farm, Deerfield Road, Water Mill.

I rushed out of the Southampton Library with notes from my research to make the 6:00 p.m. meeting at the Southampton Town Hall. I had been reading town records from the 1640's, noting the many references to Thomas Halsey and Christopher Foster. Sometimes these two stalwart farmers showed up as jurors or witnesses in court trials. Sometimes, too, Thomas showed up as a defendant for his "irreverent" outbursts during meetings. It was a cool spring evening in April, exceptionally quiet, lit by a baleful crescent moon. Still suspended in the 17th century, I walked down Jobs Lane and looked up at the same moon and smelled the same sweet, early spring breeze that Thomas and Christopher had appreciated.

The meeting's agenda was one I cared about: the board and interested locals had gathered to discuss a proposal for preserving the town's dwindling acres of farmland. I was one of the last to arrive and took a seat in back. Glancing around the small but packed room, I exchanged smiles with Lee Foster, Tom and John Halsey, their distant cousin John v.H. Halsey and Harry Ludlow. In six minutes and half a mile, I had gone from reading about the town meetings of a colonial settlement to a live town meeting 360 years later, with the same families' ancestors reiterating many of the same concerns.

The first time I saw John and Evelyn Halseys' Whitecap Farm in Water Mill, I walked through their front gates over the cattle guard into the most immaculately cared-for yard I had ever seen. It was a warm Sunday afternoon in early September. A hush lay over the courtyard, like the hush in a church. As it rolled down to Mecox Bay the farm looked like Eden tamed.

Some of the John Halseys' 65-acre farm is occupied by 10,000 small apple trees, lined up like well-behaved school children. The trees are much older than their size would imply. John, Evelyn and their two daughters, Amy and Jennifer, grow a curator's selection of apples from far-away places: New Zealand, Japan, Western Australia and more. They have names like Braeburn, Fuji, Mutsu, Winesap, Pink Lady, Jonagold, and a score of others. Some of these apple trees are 22 years old. Like Bonsais they have been meticulously pruned and trained into small graceful figures that produce an astonishingly bountiful crop. A greenhouse, pear trees, blueberry bushes, and pumpkin vines share the rest of the land, along with a small pond that is home to geese, ducks and swans, wide-mouthed bass, snapping turtles and muskrats.

When I first met John, I stopped in my tracks about ten feet away, as he surveyed me from head to toe. He has the look and bearing of a colonial farmer from the 17th century, though he dresses in Levis and Patagonia. His attention never wavers as he addresses you, slowly and deliberately, his voice warm and gentle with a slight New England accent. Paul Corwith says of John, "He doesn't talk much but when he does, you want to listen." I trudged up his back steps moaning about the countless winter days ahead of us, to which he responded, "All weather is good." His aphorisms, one of which always seems to be at hand, tend to express an acceptance of things we can't change. For any farming family, I'd realized by now, survival depends on knowing what it can't change. But also when to adapt.

John's brother Tom and his wife Dot live a short drive away on a farm on Deerfield Road, in Water Mill. An intricate network of greenhouses stretches along the western border of 75 acres of land that was first farmed by the brothers' ancestor Lemuel in about 1744. Tom and Dot have lived in the property's 1872 farmhouse since they were married in 1967. They have two children, Adam and Jocelyn. In addition to the farm, they run a summer farm stand, which began as vegetables on a card table but is now a handsome wood building, its front side open and welcoming, at the juncture of Deerfield and Head Of Pond Road. Near it stands an enormous new storage barn and an osprey nest that Tom built to help out a pair of birds he saw eating fish in his field one day.

John and his brother Tom have patrician good looks, and in many ways look alike, though Tom is more apt than John to regard a stranger with a skeptical half-smile. Both brothers have a strong faith and are philosophers as well as pragmatists. Neither is particularly vain. When I asked them why they both had the same haircut style with bangs, they looked at me blankly. John asked, "I have bangs?" and then ran his hand through his hair as if feeling it for the first time.

Everett Halsey with Potato crop, circa 1940, Whitecap Farm

One of their earliest known forebears was Thomas Halsey, born in about 1593 — exact date unknown – in Hertsfortshire County, England. His father was a yeoman in the tiny village of Flamstead which, like most villages of the time, had a common, a church, and a main street lined with houses. This village plan was the model for innumerable colonial settlements, including Southampton, Long Island. Bucolic as the original was, Tom sold his 11 acres on April 28, 1638, and took his wife, Elizabeth Wheeler, along with four of their children, on a ship across the Atlantic Ocean. He was 46 years old.

The family landed at Boston, then traveled to Lynn, Massachusetts, where they endured the severe New England winters of 1638 and 1639 on 100 acres Thomas purchased there. Life was hard, but for Thomas, the cold weather wasn't nearly as chilling as the rigid church-state government of Puritan New England. Massachusetts Governor John Winthrop was too extreme for Tom. Seeking religious freedom and more fertile land, Thomas joined 17 other heads of families, including Edward Howell, Josias Stanborough, John Cooper and Job Sayre, in purchasing a small bark, and engaged Captain Daniel Howe to transport them to a new life on Long Island. They eventually settled a plantation where the present Southampton Hospital stands, later to be called 'Olde Towne'. Of that first contingent, only five made permanent homes in Southampton. Thomas Halsey was one of them. The rest moved to different parts of Long Island or farther away. During the next few years those first settlers' lands were acquired by Christopher Foster, David Corwithen (Corwith), Thomas Hildreth, Samuel Dayton, Thomas Topping, John White, and other settlers whose names are familiar today.

In 1649, the list of Southampton townsmen numbered 29, along with their families. It was in this year that possibly the first terrible crime occurred: the apparent murder of Mrs. Elizabeth Halsey, Thomas' wife, by Indians. Sketchy historical records and folklore suggest the criminals were apprehended with the help of the sachem Wyandanch, as well as Lyon Gardiner (whose ancestors still own Gardiner's Island) and found to be Pequot Indians. They were supposedly condemned by the courts in Hartford and executed there. Thomas did remarry, although not until he was about 66 years old. With his new bride, the widow Ann Johnes, he signed an early pre-nuptial agreement to keep their estates separate for their children's sake. His son Thomas, Jr. married a cousin, Mary, and moved to land in Sagaponack that Mary's father provided. Thomas and Mary proceeded to raise 12 children: the forebears of most of the Halseys who live in the Hamptons, and beyond, today.

By the time of his death at age of 84 or 85 on August 27, 1678, Thomas had come to own various properties from Quogue (Quaquanantuck) to Sagaponack. These were divided among his three sons, Thomas Jr., Isaac and Daniel. As was customary at the time, and not uncommon today, Thomas' daughters were left no land because, it was presumed, they would obtain it by marriage. For the next eleven generations, the Halseys were concentrated mostly in Southampton, Water Mill and Mecox, and became one of the largest families in the area. By 1862 there were 42 Halsey heads of families holding 3,261 acres in Southampton Town. Today that number is about the same, but most of these families' land was sold long ago. Today, John and Tom's families are among the largest landholders of the group.

The hardiest of the Long Island farmers, like the Halseys, survived by diversifying their crops. Most of the present-day Thomas' 75 acres, called Halsey Farm and Nursery, are planted with an extensive variety of vegetables and flowers which are sold at the farm stand on their property. In addition, Thomas has three acres under greenhouse glass where annual and perennial flowers are grown to sell in the spring. John and his family have added a peach orchard and a greenhouse full of flowers to their Whitecap Farm.

John and Tom, along with their sisters Margaret and Nancy, were all born and raised one house east from where John now lives, on the corner of Horse Mill Lane in Water Mill. On this land, their father, Everett, grew 200 acres of potatoes. Everett bought his first tractor in the 1920's, a Fordson, and their first mechanical potato harvester in 1957. Before then, horses did the work of pulling plows and dragging potato diggers. Potatoes were culled from the soil by these rudimentary machines and then picked up by hand and loaded onto trucks in baskets or bags.

Tom remembers first learning how to disc a field, (the final stage of finely pulverizing soil between metal discs), then plow, (a much more technically difficult process where the soil is actually turned over, so care must be taken not to change the levelness of the field.) He and John both helped their father farm potatoes until they went to college. When I asked Tom and John what they did for fun growing up, they said they would rush home from school to be on the farm because there was, as Tom put it, "unlimited fun on the farm." Besides driving tractors, they would cut down cars and turn them into "hot rods," one of which Tom drove to high school. They spent a lot of time on the bay, hunting ducks or geese, or fishing by haul seine, and putting down eel pots. In winter they would trap muskrats. Until they got their own ice boats, they would fix a sail to just about anything: old cars, wagons, even their American Flexible Flyer sleds, and steer them across the ice. Whenever the boys told their father they'd finished their work for the day and were headed down to the bay, he would say, "Let me make something clear, there is always more work to do on a farm but if you feel alright about leaving it for now, then O.K." So off they'd go.

From their father, the Halsey boys learned the same values that have been passed down through the family for hundreds of years. Their father taught them that honesty is paramount and that your word is invaluable, so make it count and don't give it carelessly. They both love the independence of life on a farm and the fact that every day is different. "Nature is so unpredictable," is Tom's aphorism for it, "and therefore always challenging and instructive." Besides, he says, "you just can't walk away from a farm when you've grown up on one."

John went to college to study dairy science, then came back home and bought cows to start his own dairy business. He met his future wife at a dance in 1966 near Southampton College, which she was attending at the time. Evelyn looked, John recalls, "as out of place as I felt," and so he went up and introduced himself. When he showed her his farm, Evelyn knew this was where she wanted to be. Her future seemed laid out perfectly before her. When I asked her if she ever regretted her choice, she said emphatically, "Oh my gosh no. Never."

Evelyn loved doing everything. She drove the tractors. She mucked out cow stalls. Manual labor didn't bother her at all. She found nature fascinating as well as a great instructor. "Nature tells you everything you need to know." The Halseys soon had fifty cows and a milking parlor, which John built. Evelyn loved helping the cows give birth, the calves so clean and soft and new smelling. The farm helped define her philosophies and faith.

One month after they married they opened their first Milk Pail farm stand, in a tiny rented building at the corner of Montauk Highway and Hayground Road, to sell the milk from their dairy. The shop prospered, but both John and Evelyn eventually found the dairy business onerous and financially draining. After nine years, John realized he had to sell his cows or go broke. With their proceeds from the sale, he and Evelyn bought four acres from John's uncle David on Montauk Highway. With hardly any capital left, they built the present Milk Pail store themselves, inside and out. Evelyn would be up on the rafters pounding nails and John's mother, Kay, would be watching her from below, worrying about her. John built everything by hand. Every door, drawer or work surface of this beloved Water Mill institution was meticulously designed to be as useful and practical as possible.

A first time visitor to the Milk Pail may wonder how a Hamptons roadside stand came to sell maple syrup and cheddar cheese. Both come from the Vermont farm to which Evelyn's parents had moved. The first apples came from Vermont, too. Soon the apples and cider were selling so well that the Halseys began planting their own apple trees. Learning as they went, they diversified by growing exotic strains instead of the common grocery store varieties.

John and Evelyn had two daughters, Amy and Jenn. John had grown up believing that farming was a man's job. He learned very quickly that he didn't need a son. His girls made up for any lack of brute strength with their resourcefulness, creativity and good sense. Amy's fondest early memories are of working with her dad, riding on the equipment, and just reveling in the soil. Her close

Everett Halsey digging potatoes, late 1920's, Whitecap Farm.

family and the knowledge that she always had a future on the farm gave her a sense of place in the world. She still finds work dictated by the seasons to be reassuring. Today she works in tandem with her sister Jenn, each working on the other's days off. The drawback is they don't spend much time off together.

Amy is the most artistic member of her family, and has developed a successful flower growing and design business over the past six years from greenhouses on the farm. She's taken several trips to Holland as part of an internship to study and learn more about greenhouse flowers. She holds two degrees from Cobleskill, in Floriculture and Plant Science. Her greatest satisfaction comes from caring for bulbs, cuttings and seedlings and seeing them grow into gorgeous flowers. Jenn works closely with her father, caring for the apple orchards, pumpkin patch, blueberries and the peach orchard next to the Milk Pail, which she first planted in 1997. She holds a degree in agriculture from Cornell and was the first farmer from Long Island to win the Young Farmer/Rancher Achievement Award for New York State in 1999. Jenn puts her creative talents to use solving problems on the farm, whether it's fixing a tractor or trying out new growing or pest management ideas.

John's brother Tom and his wife Dot first met in kindergarten in Bridgehampton. She grew up in a house on Edgewood Avenue and they would see each other at school or parties. There were beach parties to go to, sailing in the summer, ice boating in the winter, and the Candy Kitchen, which in the 1950's was the center of activity on Main Street. After they married, Dot taught home economics but stopped when she had her children, Jocelyn and Adam. Dot has the dulcet voice of a young girl; the first time I phoned the farm, she answered and I almost asked to speak to her mother.

Tom grew potatoes until the early 1970's, when he and Dot started shifting over to greenhouse-grown flowers and vegetables. Tom built the Halsey Farm Stand himself in 1994. The family business now is more interesting, but also more complex, than when the fields yielded a single crop. Both Dot and Tom work weekends, along with their son Adam and his wife Beth. Dot works the retail side of their business, the one job Tom tries his best to avoid. He's been known to say on the rare occasion that he's been cornered by a customer, "Oh sorry, I only sweep around here and do the plumbing. I don't know anything about these plants. Go ask that lady over there." Then he motions to where Dot is standing. Once, when a customer wandered into a clearly roped-off area of the greenhouse, he turned the sprinkler system on.

Adam has always wanted to be a farmer. He has blue eyes as clear as a July sky and the flawless manners of an 18th century gentleman. By five or six he was already cultivating corn and spreading fertilizer. His only doubts came in his last two years of college, when all his friends were going off to jobs somewhere else. The wistfulness he felt made him realize he had to be sure of what he wanted to do. But once he came back to the family farm, he never doubted his decision. Each day is different. One day he's a blacksmith, the next a carpenter or mechanic. Always, he's a farmer. Adam is the 12th generation of a farming tradition, the eighth generation to work the same land. He often finds artifacts in the soil, parts of ancient tools and equipment his forbears used.

Adam feels optimistic about the future and believes there will always be farming but farmers, he feels, must be willing to change. "Anything I have to do to survive as a farmer," he says, "I'm willing to do." Adam married Beth, a dairy farmer's daughter and granddaughter, after college graduation. Beth enjoys working on the Halsey farm, but has found catering to weekenders from the city a culture shock. She's taken over much of the plant ordering and scheduling, as well as all the bill paying and bookkeeping.

What Tom loves most about farming is the smell of the first plowed spring soil. It smells of all the green promise stored there for millions of years, ready to be fulfilled again and again by capable hands. Tom and John's father Everett once said a man is "born a farmer, not made a farmer." Both brothers feel that farming is much more than a chosen occupation. It is a part of their overall faith, and makes them feel they're part of something bigger than themselves. Their hearts and souls have become inseparable from the natural world that unfolds before them every day. Over the years, walking his farm each day, John has come to realize, he says, that we are only temporary caretakers of the land. As his knowledge of nature grows, so does his feeling of insignificance in the larger scheme of things.

Both families have identical goals for the future. Each wants to have their children, the 12th generation of the Halsey family in America, inherit the farms as was the case with Tom and John. In their current incarnation, the potential federal inheritance taxes present a major hurdle. Previous generations were able to pass on their farms because their value, even as developed land, was not so out of proportion to their use as farms. Today the Internal Revenue Service taxes land on the basis of its "highest value use." In the Hamptons, that use, based on the residential zoning of the property, is both obvious and inexorable. Land for housing sells in this rarefied enclave for $1 million or more an acre when the land is subdivided into one- or two-acre lots. So a farm of, say, 70 acres close to the Atlantic Ocean may appear, to the IRS, to be worth $70 million, less the cost of development. Federal inheritance taxes, as high as 55%, are levied accordingly. Needless to say, many East End farms have been lost due to these taxes, or the anticipation of them in the future.

One way to avoid the full brunt of such a tax bill is to gift the farm to the next generation over decades through limited partnerships and the like. This requires tremendous foresight, sophisticated estate planning, not to mention the acceptance of one's own mortality. Failing that, parents can donate all or most of the development rights (i.e. the right to build houses) to a land trust or municipality. But when a family's equity is tied up in land, that's easier said than done. A variation on this theme is to sell the development rights at full value or at a bargain price. While this doesn't solve the inheritance tax problem, it assures the protection of the farm, or a portion thereof, and provides the farm family with liquidity.

A welcomed proposal by the Peconic Land Trust has been to defer federal inheritance taxes unless and until the farm is developed or sold for that purpose. Legislation has been introduced in Congress to this end, but it has a long way to go. In the final analysis, farm families that own land of high residential value must grapple with the future of their farms. Failing that, their only choice, when that fateful time comes, may be to sell off a sizable portion of the farm, if not all of it, in order to pay top-tier taxes on the rest. That, of course, will assure that the 14th or 15th generation has virtually no land left to farm. Clearly, the system needs fixing. As Tom Halsey puts it, " the sale of the land should be the trigger for inheritance tax, not the inheritance tax triggering the sale." Both sets of parents are doing what they can, giving their children as much land each year as legally possible without triggering huge taxes, but that process won't allow the passing down of a significant portion of their farms in time to avoid the huge financial obstacle. All the Halseys can do is keep farming and hope that conservation-minded lawmakers bring some sense to the tax laws while the farm is intact. Otherwise, the land and its produce, the family heritage and equity, built up over 350 years, will be gone forever.

Threshing grain at Halsey Farm, circa 1880.

THE FOSTER FAMILY

Charles Foster, 1965, Sagaponack.

It was by accident that I happened to wander down the Fosters' long dirt driveway to the back of their family farm. I was there to ask a farming question for a friend, but as I looked for someone to talk to, my eye drew me farther on until I stood alone in their back shop yard, towered over by huge machines, mute as dinosaur exhibits. Massive silver silos and half-moon roofed buildings rose against a field of the tallest corn I had ever seen, golden-green in the mid-August dusk. Entranced, I wondered how I had driven by this farm a hundred times and never known the beautiful, hidden world that existed here.

When I asked Jimmy Comfort at the farm where I could find Dean Foster he answered with the first of many "farmer directions." "He's harvesting grain across from Dayton's farm." When I asked him where Dayton's farm was he replied, "Across from Conklin's." After several seconds, in response to my blank look he offered, " Take the headland across Kinkade's through the wildflower field and you'll see him." And then finally, "I'll drive you."

From the headland I could see a huge red machine moving through ripe rye in a cloud of dust and bits of chaff. Dean was at the wheel and when I waved he came to a halt and signaled me to come aboard. I yelled to him over the roar of the combine within the driver's cab, "you have the best job in the world!" "Yeah I do," he yelled back, "but I wish I had another 200 acres to harvest this morning." Dean and his father Cliff had just received the "Century Farm Award" from the New York State Agricultural Society for farming the same land continually for 100 years.

Both the Foster and the Halsey families, I learned, were among the first settlers of Southampton in the 1640's. Both surnames are listed in heraldry books as having a "Coat of Arms". (Heraldic arms were not, in fact, badges of aristocracy, but rather honors attesting to the bearer's acts of bravery, heroism or self-sacrifice.) The first Foster on the East End of Long Island was Christopher Foster, who was born in Ewell, Surrey in 1603. There is a record of him along with other English fishermen visiting the northern shores of Cape Cod and Maine before 1628. He left England at the age of 32 with his wife Frances and three young children. Two years later, in 1637, he was listed as a freeman—landowner and voter – in Boston and owner of 60 acres nearby in Lynn. Yet like Thomas Halsey, he longed to be free of the colony's stern Puritanism, and so resettled for a time in Hempstead, Long Island, known then as the Hempstead Plains, where most of the livestock from Shinnecock west was grazed. In 1650 he moved to Southampton where he was elected "townsman" to help manage the town's affairs. He lived on Main Street and attended town meetings with settlers whose names adorn street signs today: White, Sayre, Dayton and Topping. In l653, he and Thomas Halsey were listed as members of a "Squadron for cutting up whales that might drift up upon the shores." In February, the following year, because he held Proprietor's rights he took part in the divisions of the common lands including Sagaponack. Out of forty-one lots Christopher drew #27. Thomas Halsey drew #13 and John White #6. There is no known map of these divisions available today.

Cliff Foster, Christopher's descendant and the eleventh generation in America, is a big man. He is 6' 2" but loses 1" to a slight forward tilt earned from two hip replacement surgeries. He was born in 1939 to Charles and Anne Hedges Foster of Sagaponack, and now lives across the street in his great-grandfather Josiah's house on forty acres near Sagg Pond, in Sagaponack. He's gentle and direct, so direct that he pins you with his gaze. Keenly intelligent, he takes pleasure in figuring out any imaginable mechanical challenge of farming and home repair. As I walked around his shop peering into cabinet after cabinet of flat red drawers filled with the most amazing looking tools, I exclaimed "it looks like you could build an airplane in here." "Oh that would be easy," he replied. As a singular example of self-sufficiency the family does all its own plumbing and electrical work. The Fosters help neighbors in need, too. One March day a nor'easter pounded the Hamptons. I ventured out, not expecting to find anyone. As I drove by the Foster Farm I saw a flurry of activity. The electricity was down and all the food in the Sagaponack General Store, a fixture since the early 1900's, was going to go bad unless something was done to revive the refrigerators. The Fosters were all engaged in repairing the store's busted generator while loaning the owners one of their own to keep the food cold.

Beach buggies on Sagg Beach, 1959.   Looking north from Sagg Beach, 1959.

The Foster Family and baby Clifford, 1939,
Foster Farm, Sagaponack.

Isabel Beattie and Dorothy Anderson at the beach shack, 1948,
Sagg Beach.

It was Cliff's father Charles who taught him mechanics. "If you want to make it as a farmer you have to do your own mechanical work." I asked Cliff if he had gone to college for engineering; like his father, he'd only completed high school. This didn't seem to limit either man. From his mother, Anne, he learned the difference between right and wrong and because his father always told him that "you can learn something from any fool" he has always been able to talk and listen to anyone. Paul Corwith said of Cliff "He must love farming because he could have done anything he wanted."

Cliff's first job on the farm was picking vegetables, which he says he hated, but soon enough he was plowing, discing and running the grain combine. His family raised a dozen beef cattle and laying chickens which they shared with family and friends. They were essentially self-sufficient, growing or raising all their own food — especially during WWII when all they bought from stores was sugar and sometimes bread. He recalls that there were delicious grapes in Montauk to pick and cranberry bogs in Napeague, and they would fish for 'Bottle Fish' off Long Beach in Sag Harbor, also known as Foster Memorial Beach, which was given to the Town of Southampton by Charles and his brother Everett. I asked Cliff if he'd ever wanted for anything when he was a child and he replied, "never." At that point in our interview his black lab Raisin came out from behind a drill press and sheepishly placed her head in Cliff's lap. "My father used to say a man with one dog is a wise man, but a man with two is a fool." He paused, then added, "I wonder what he thought of me when I had four?"

When younger, Cliff made beach buggies from junk cars. In the winter when he wasn't iceboating, he went sledding on Noyack Golf Course. Among his friends were Bud Topping, Pete and Paul Corwith and Tom and John L. Halsey. John dated Cliff's sister, Julia. The local meeting place was the Candy Kitchen on Main Street Bridgehampton and even today, if you drive by before it opens at 7:00 you might catch a glimpse of farmers using their own private key to let themselves in, to make coffee, helping themselves to a danish and leaving payment in the cash register drawer. Looking for a partner in life, Cliff had to look no further than Sagaponack to find Lee. Her upper-middle-class New Jersey family spent each summer in a beach shack by Fairfield Pond, furnished with whatever happened to wash up on shore.

After the hurricane of 1938, which placed the Beattie shack in the middle of the pond, Cliff's father Charles let Lee's father John move the shack to the beach at the end of Sagg Main Street. Lee spent her summers exploring the vast Sagaponack fields, ponds and ocean beaches. She rode on the back of Bud Topping's tractor, had the privilege of riding the horses at Stevenson's, the only two stabled in Sagaponack at the time. Lee watched the young farmers cooling themselves off at the end of hot summer days and envisioned herself someday living in Sagg, instead of her very separate life in New Jersey.

One fall Lee headed off for college – in Texas, at her mother's insistence, perhaps so that Lee might forget Cliff. One year later Cliff proposed and Lee accepted. From that moment they were in a contract to keep their farm and family thriving. Cliff cut part of a Farm Journal article out called "What it means to be a farm wife," and even though Lee found it hilarious she kept it in her wallet. Part of it read; "there will be a time when you will have needs of your own and you'll just have to put your sturdy oxfords down.." She had three children, Robin, Dean and Marilee, each two years apart, and felt at times too young for such an undertaking. But today she is a confident woman, still compelled by the issues of farmland conservation.

When I first spoke to Lee we sat in her kitchen. It's a room with two tall glass doors that frame the sunset at the end of each day. While we talked, each hour was heralded by the song of a different bird from a clock on the wall. At one point she wondered aloud if she'd married Cliff...or the land. But since Cliff is the land, we agreed, she really married both.

Lee Beattie and Clifford Foster, 1963.

Lee's mother, Isabel Beattie, 1949, Sagaponack.

Robin Foster is the oldest child and, as is the case in most young families, she faced the greatest challenges. From an early age her interest diverged and focused on horses. Her parents did not discourage her but did insist she help out on the farm when she was growing up. Today she has her own home and a business training and kenneling dogs. She's also an accomplished carriage driver, winning competitions around the country with Morgan horses, having been set on her way when she hitched her first horse to a breaking cart. She remains very close to her family and supports her younger brother and sister in their desire to continue farming. I've had Thanksgiving dinner at the farm in Sagaponack more than once and marveled at what an egalitarian family the Fosters are, all interesting and interested in each other. Someone is always jumping up to grab the dictionary or encyclopedia to verify a fact or answer a question brought up by their arcane dinner conversations.

Dean and Marilee look like twins even though they're two years apart. They grew up working and playing together on the farm and at times seem to be able to read each other's minds. Dean is confident and straightforward, like his father, and Marilee is contemplative and erudite like her mother. Dean never went to college, knowing his life was on the farm. Marilee went to Beloit College and studied fine art. She is a painter, sculptress and accomplished writer with her own newspaper column and a published book about farm life in the Hamptons. Marilee also manages to run a vegetable stand in between the many responsibilities she shares with her father and Dean. She grows a wide variety of vegetables but specializes in rare and eccentric heirloom tomatoes, with names like Black Krim, Aunt Ruby's Green German, White Wonder and Caspian Pink. Each selection is accompanied by a tiny anthropomorphic portrait of the relevant vegetable that the stand is famous for. She and Dean have also become entrepreneurs, creating their own line of delicious, natural potato chips made from their own crop, in a small factory established in what was once a potato storage barn.

Across the street from Cliff and Lee's house is Cliff's childhood home. Dean and his new wife Dorian live there now. Dean feels blessed to have a father who has so much knowledge about farming, business and mechanics. He says that that knowledge, coupled with his father's imagination and vision, created a world without limits. Problems were opportunities in search of solutions, and this freedom is Dean's greatest reward. He has a strong spiritual connection to his farming heritage and the first European settlers who laid the groundwork for this country gained through their labors. Family is the most important element in his life and he wants his children to have the same knowledge and opportunities that he has had.

Today the Fosters cultivate 450 acres of land that they either own or lease. They rotate the fields each year with potatoes and field corn. Marilee's vegetables, flowers and berries are grown on the farm in a field behind Lee and Cliff's house. Cliff is an accomplished farmer. An employee of many years, "Jigger" Howe, put it one day at their farm, "Cliff has forgotten more about corn than most people will ever know."

Along with the other remaining farm families on the East End, the Fosters face the same obstacles jeopardizing their efforts to pass their farm to the next generation. In anticipation of a huge inheritance tax bill the Fosters are utilizing their right to gift land to Dean and Marilee and Robin. They are also selling the development rights to provide liquidity, lower the value of their land and subsequently lower the potential tax burden. The value of these restricted lands, however, is climbing daily and soon will present its own tax burdens. The family continues to farm and weigh their options for the future, while working for amendments to the tax laws which directly affect their ability to pass down the farm to heirs or those willing to continue.

As I bid goodbye to Cliff on my most recent visit, I turned to ask him if he thought we were headed for a bitter cold end to what had been an unusually mild winter. "Lord only knows," Cliff said, "and he's never sure."

Isabel Beattie, circa 1940, Sagaponack.

THE CORWITH FAMILY

Pete and Paul's great aunts, circa 1890.

Paul Corwith explained that it took twelve oxen to haul the wind mill in pieces from Hog Neck, today called North Haven, twelve miles to the Town Common in Water Mill where it can still be seen today. It had been built in 1800 and fourteen years later it was purchased by James Corwith, Paul's Great-Great-Grandfather for $750 so he could begin earning a living grinding grain. Paul opened the door to the mill with his own key and took me inside. The mill had just been entirely renovated with contributions from residents to ensure its continued survival as the most prominent landmark in Water Mill. He explained the intricate workings of the mill and showed me where someone in the 1800's had carved by hand into a beam, "Began To Grind August 1, 1800".

Paul, along with all the Corwith men, is handsome in a rugged way that comes from a life spent out in the sun. He lives just south of the Water Mill family farm, in a ranch house he built in 1960. He loves the farming life and the many challenges it presents throughout any given year. One of its most important lessons, he says, is how to live with unpredictability. Growing up was a wonderful time, despite the Second World War and its deprivations. The family would gather together for picnics to share the local bounty of clams from Shinnecock Bay and pickerel and bass from the nearby Mill Pond. A great sorrow for Paul was the death of his brother Pete from cancer a decade ago, an enormous blow to the family, but Paul, his son Mark and Pete's son Dicky pooled their efforts and kept the farm going.

As I stood on the corner of the family farm, framed by the intersection of Head of the Pond Road and Water Mill Towd Road, a workman at the farm motioned across the street when I asked where Dicky Corwith, Pete's son, was. I could see him from where I stood, a shock of light blond hair and impenetrable sunglasses. He was talking, giving instructions to someone, as he watched me cross the street. A six foot tall, perfect replica of a wind mill drew my eye westward where it crowned the triangle point of their farm. He looked careworn. When I asked him what he liked most about farming he said, "Oh, it's all mostly just a misery." I wasn't sure if he was kidding me or not so I questioned him further. "Well then why do you continue?" "What else would I do?" was his immediate reply and then he checked himself, "I guess like any other job it has its good days and its bad. " " Today is a bad day?" I asked, to which he smiled and said "You guessed right."

We were in the midst of a summer drought worse than any that even the oldest farmers could remember. It was mid-July and Dicky and Mark were only able to irrigate 55 of 250 acres of potatoes they were growing because there were no nearby water hook-ups to most of their fields. They felt deeply discouraged watching acre after acre of young plants burn with each passing day. Eventually the rains did come and their crop was saved, but this is the kind of anxiety that can grind on these farmers any given year. Too little rain one year, too much the next: a farmer who's not stoic and steadfast won't last.

Mark Corwith, Paul's son and Dicky's cousin, was working in their farm shop on a broken piece of equipment. Farm shops are interesting places, filled with generations of tools, fabricating machinery, farm equipment parts and all manner of gadgets. Some were bought, some traded for and many are hand hewn, each with its own purpose. Farmers today remain as inventive as their predecessors; if there isn't a machine or piece of equipment suited for the task, they'll make one. The wood planks of the barn walls were barely visible beneath hanging tools, vintage potato bags and old and new photographs, each generation of farmers adding to this evocative collage. The ubiquitous "Babe" calendar was securely hung in a prominent spot by the phone where hours are spent ordering seed, fertilizer and other supplies or searching for parts.

Dicky and Mark's ancestor Digory, also written Dickery and Digeren, was born in 1580 in Cornwall, England and died in Boston in July of 1653. He became a ship master on vessels bound for New England. He had at least one son, David, who was born in 1610. That son married Grace Alcock and had eight children: the progenators of the Corwith clan. Subsequent generations are mired in geneological chaos, however, because the Corwiths, like many New England families, exhibited a striking lack of imagination in naming their children. By the fourth generation, half a dozen brothers and cousins appear in the family records with the same

Peach baskets at Corwith stand on Montauk Highway, Water Mill, 1948.   Potato harvest, circa 1940.

Potato bags on the way to market, 1940's.

Christian name. There is a David Corwith listed in 1639 as living in Taunton, Massachusetts and he may have been the same David Corwith who was High Sheriff at Marblehead. In 1649, David was listed as a member of the church at Salem. One of these Davids - or the same one, after vigorous peregrinations - moved at some point to Southold, Long Island where his will is dated August 30, 1665.

Corwith brothers and cousins settled in a wide range from Huntington, New York, Sussex County, Delaware to Elizabeth, New Jersey. The earliest available record of a Corwith in Southampton is Caleb, listed in the Southampton Town Records as having accommodations in North Sea in 1661 and a homestead west of Snake Hollow, north of County Road. Caleb, and a brother David shared the responsibilities of managing the Town along with Thomas Halsey and Christopher Foster in the 1660's.

For the next one hundred and fifty years, the Corwith family grew deeper roots in Bridgehampton, Mecox and Water Mill. Three Corwith men served in Capt. David Pierson's Company during the Revolutionary War. James, the Corwith who bought the wind mill, had seven children, only two of whom survived, Caleb and Samuel. Caleb was noted in the New Haven records of 1654 for complaints made against him and a brother or cousin Phillip for traveling (on horseback) on the Sabbath. They were pursuing a man who owed them a considerable amount of money and was attempting to leave for Virginia. Samuel was the adventurous one, joining the California gold rush and, atypically, having some luck. When he returned home he took over his father's mill, ran a general store in Water Mill, and served as postmaster. Of his five children, the only surviving boy was James Hervey, who grew up to work a 25-acre farm on Head of Pond Road that he had bought with the money he made from the sale of his father's general store. One of his sons, James Carlton, expanded the farm to some 125 acres of wheat, corn and potatoes. And when James Carlton died in 1966, his sons Pete and Paul took over.

Pete and Paul both grew up in a home next to the farm house that Pete's son Dicky now lives in on Head of Pond Road in Water Mill. Along with potatoes the brothers raised as many as 3,000 laying hens and also grew peaches. Pete married Marilyn Palmer on June 7, 1952 and together they had four children, Emily, Lynn, Richard (Dicky) and Bill. "Pete was as honest as the day is long," Cliff Foster recalls of the brother who died of cancer. Paul married Norma Keuogh on May 4, 1957 and they also had four children, Gail, Mark, David and Doreen. Norma died in a car accident in 1998, a terrible shock and loss for her family. Marilyn Corwith, Pete's widow and Dicky's mother, lives across the street from the farm in a home that they built in 1956. When I interviewed her we sat in her kitchen. At one hour intervals a different bird sang out its song from a clock on her kitchen wall— the same clock that fills Lee Foster's kitchen with bird calls at the stroke of each hour. Marilyn met Pete at her sister's wedding. Becoming a farmer's wife was not a difficult transition because her family always had a huge vegetable garden from which they canned all their vegetables. She easily took the responsibility of running the Corwith stand selling peaches harvested from acres of peach trees.

Dicky was 37 when his father Pete passed away. He and his Uncle Paul asked Paul's son Mark to join them, taking Pete's place in their partnership. Mark had his own landscaping business at the time but decided to put that aside. They focused on growing potatoes and corn which had become the big crops on Long Island by the 1950's. They graded their own potatoes and those of other farmers and began selling to grocery store chains such as A&P in 1952. They cultivated about 600 acres, half of which they owned and the other half they leased. Dicky married Robin Fenner, a Connecticut tomboy who had come to Water Mill to escape the quotidian existence of the suburbs. They have two children, Richard and Christina. Rich has been working at his father's side since he was able to stand up. His love of the farm will carry him through the inevitable trials every farmer experiences.

Mark also grows a wide variety of flowering stock and evergreens on a fifty-acre nursery where the families' peach trees once stood. He propagates much of his stock in a greenhouse at the farm. Like the Halseys and the Fosters, Mark loves the smell of the first plowed earth in spring, the variety of jobs and the fact that every day is different. He likes being his own boss and has learned that you have to treat a farm like any other business and "You can't let too much bother you." He married Jill Loweth, a Long Island girl, whom he met here one summer. They have three children, Travis, Samantha and Kelly. Mark hopes one of his children will decide to continue in their father's footsteps. So far Travis' interests lie in computer technology, but perhaps one of the girls will join in as Marilee Foster or the Halsey girls have. They will not be pressured into it by their parents, however, who believe each child should make his or her own decision about the future.

Each spring Dicky and Mark buy six Hereford cows which they butcher in the late fall to provide beef for their families and friends. I happened to stop by the farm the morning they were preparing to butcher the cows. As I prepared to leave, not wanting to be around for the event, I asked Dicky "Do you think they know what's about to happen?" He shook his head. "No," he replied, "I don't tell them."

I spent an afternoon immersed in past generations as I flipped through letters in a box stored at an old Corwith house that belongs to the Bridgehampton Historical Society. The house was built by Henry Corwith in 1860. The letters are all written with a quill in an elegant script, each letter set off with flourishes, the lines all perfectly straight. I paused at one letter written from Jacksonville, Florida in February of 1848. It begins, "Dear Parents" and is written by David Corwith, son of William and Hannah (Halsey) Corwith of Bridgehampton. He tells them that the warm weather is helping his throat and that he feels well enough to have ridden his horse ten miles that day. He mentions that the southern plum and peach trees are in bloom and when he rode through the woods he found violets and jasmine. He intends to return home in March, he adds longingly, and looks forward to being once again among his friends on the "Green Isle."

I put the letter aside and picked up the next one, also from Jacksonville but penned in a different hand. A woman had written it in 1649 to Mrs. William Corwith, sending condolences upon the recent death of her son David, in Jacksonville. Those two letters traced the arc of a life, one filled with hope and longing and cherished details. It was a life, in truth, lost to time, except as a link in the chain of a family: a family whose descendants, David would be happy to know, are still on the Green Isle working the land, 150 years later.

Pete Corwith ice boating, 1940's, Mill Pond.

THE ZALUSKI FAMILY

Bill "The Colonel" Zaluski aboard a F20 Farmall tractor, circa 1938, Zaluski Farm,
Deerfield Road, Water Mill.

It was Tom Halsey's idea to ask the Zaluskis to be the fourth family featured in this book. "You better talk to his wife first," he said as he pointed to their farm, just north from where we stood on the Halsey farm. "If Bill sees you, he's liable to run you off the place." With trepidation, I drove to the Zaluski Farm.

Bill and Joan Zaluski's home stands, iconic, on a crest of a hill on Deerfield road, surrounded by 70 acres of farmland. The drive leading to the quintessential, white clapboard farmhouse is flanked with signs admonishing drivers to 'DRIVE SLOW,' to heed 'CHILDREN AND DOGS AT PLAY,' and to not exceed '5 MILES PER HOUR.' My car crept up the driveway. I was hoping I might catch Joan first when I saw Bill emerge from the shadow of the garage walking briskly straight for me. When he reached me he greeted me most pleasantly. I realized Tom had played a farmer's joke on me – not the first and not the last. Bill's flannel shirt and mechanic's pants had been roughly stitched here and there and the skin on his neck and hands had deep brown furrows like a spring farm field. I introduced myself and explained that I hoped he'd be part of the picture-and-essay book I was planning. He thought for a moment and said " Well that sounds alright to me, as long as you don't take my picture."

Bill Zaluski at 75 is at once all the ages he's ever been: full of the irrepressible mischief of a teenager even as he dispenses the wisdom and tenderness of his years. Whenever he caught sight of me, he would raise his fist in mock threat, or shake his head in feigned disgust at the sight of "the girl with her God damn cameras." Then he'd smile and ask, "Where ya been Sunny?" The first time I interviewed him he told me "There are two things about me you should know, my word is gold and I'm never late." Both are true. One of my questions that day was about his children. He and his wife Joan had four boys, he told me. "No girls," I asked. "Oh, yeah, we had two girls but I put them is a sack and tossed them in the pond so they wouldn't grow up to give some man trouble," was his reply.

I learned that what Bill Zaluski loves about farming is plowing. Especially in the spring. He couldn't put into words exactly why, just that he loves the roar of the tractor as it starts up, and loves watching the rich soil spilling away in neat furrows. "The smell of the earth and to see the ground working all the time is so great," was how he finally summed it up. The worst things about farming, for him, are the weather and the government. Both unpredictable. I once asked him what the coming spring weather was going to be like and he replied, " I have no idea, and anyone that tells you he does, doesn't know what he's talking about."

His pleasures are simple. He likes to shoot crows and every Saturday morning he likes to go to the Southampton Town Court and listen to the judge deal with the previous night's misadventures. He used to keep crab traps in Mecox Bay but no longer does because there are now too few crabs to make it worthwhile. He doesn't like eating in restaurants - "Why would I want a bunch of strangers watching me eat?" — and he doesn't socialize much. He's had two heart operations. As he explains, "the first time they sawed me in half I had to go into the city (actually Manhasset) and since I don't like to go past Riverhead (about twenty minutes west of his farm), I just lay down in the back seat until we got there."

One day while Bill and I were talking in the driveway, his wife Joan came home from running errands. They exchanged a few words about the day's events and then he said, "Go on, get in the house and do some housework before I give you the boot!" and a big grin spread across Joan's face. As she entered the house he mused, "You sleep with them, eat with them and before you know it, they think they're as good as you."

The Zaluskis are relative newcomers to Long Island farm life and, indeed, to the United States. Where the Halsey, Foster and Corwith ancestors emigrated from England to the New World and Long Island in the early 17th Century, the first standard-bearer for the Zaluski clan arrived on Long Island in the waning years of the 19th Century. Where Halseys, Fosters and Corwiths have been plowing this area's rich soil for a dozen generations, Bill Zaluski and his children are third-and fourth-generation Long Island farmers. Bill's grandfather, Tomasy Ludvik Zaluski, was born in 1865 in Zamoscie, a tiny village outside the agricultural hub of Ostroleka, in the rich, primeval forests and plains between Warsaw and Bialystok, in northeastern Poland. Tomasy, who became known as Louis after

Louis' Victorian home on north Deerfield Road,
circa 1926, Water Mill.

Louis, Anna, Stella, Stanley and William Zaluski,
circa 1903, River Head.

Leaving the Church

Spring - 1954

Joan Bennett Webber and Bill Zaluski, 1950, Southampton.   Bill plowing near Deerfield Road, 1954.

he immigrated to the United States, grew flax and other grains in and around Zamoscie and by his mid-twenties managed to purchase his own lands, unusual at that time. He lived in a home with a thatched roof, typical of the time and place, and in the late 1880's married Anna Tyzka, whose family farmed nearby. Many years later Anna told her daughters that Louis was the most elegant man she'd ever seen.

The Poland in which Louis Zaluski grew to manhood was a land of serfs and masters, beset by almost constant strife and political unrest. Prussian and Russian regimes vied for territory, each controlling large portions of the country as they strove to eradicate the traditions and national character of the people they governed. Strict sanctions were placed on the Roman Catholic Church, and monasteries were closed. In the mid-1860's, Russian became the obligatory first language in all secondary schools. Almost certainly, young Louis was required to recite the Lord's Prayer in Russian and learn to recite from memory the names of all members of the Tsar's family. With his religious and political freedoms threatened in a way that would have seemed all too familiar to the Halseys, Fosters and Corwiths of England 270 years earlier, Louis reached the same desperate conclusion they had: the New World was his only hope for a better life.

Louis sailed to America in 1896 hoping to find work, save money, and get established so that Anna and their daughter, Stella, born in 1893, could join him as soon as possible. Long Island was his destination because other Polish families, including those from his region, were already established there. They were farmers by trade and the principal commercial activity on Long Island at the turn of the century was agriculture. Within a few years of his arrival, Louis' sister and brother, Veronica and Vincent, followed him there.

The Long Island that greeted Louis in 1896 bore little resemblance to the pristine wilderness encountered by the Halseys, Fosters and Corwiths. Most of the great forests had been cleared, and farms dotted the landscape. Rail lines extended as far as Southampton and transportation to the more easterly parts of the Island was by horse-drawn carriage. Louis quickly found work on the Young potato farm in Riverhead. He was happy with the terms of his employment — $8.00 a month and a roof over his head – but potato farming at the turn of the century was a tedious, time-consuming, and backbreaking enterprise. A horse-drawn potato digger with curved tines would pull the tubers out of the ground and leave them in the furrows where cadres of stooping men would collect them into baskets and then heave them onto a waiting wagon. This grueling routine continued well into the 1950's, when the first mechanical potato harvester was invented. Fertilizer came only in 125-pound bags until the late 1970's; the bags had to be loaded and unloaded from horse-drawn wagons. Before harvesting could begin, the potato vines had to be chopped with a crude, steel-flanged device called a Roto Beater. On dry afternoons, this process would create huge clouds of dust that could be seen for miles. As Bill Zaluski says today, "You had to have a lot of bark to do that kind of work." Today a harvester, truck and potato scoop do most of it.

By 1900, Louis had managed to save enough to pay for the passage of Anna, Stella, and the newest addition to his family, Stanley, born in Poland several months after Louis emigrated. On December 29, 1900, the ship Oldenburg left Breman, Germany with Anna, who was 30 years old, and her two children. Two weeks later they were united with Louis in a small cottage provided for them by Louis' employer. In 1901, William was born. Two years after that, Anna gave birth to another daughter, Martha.

For Louis and his family, the following years were ones of inspiring progress and accomplishment. In 1908, the Zaluski family moved to a hamlet called Hay Ground, bisected by current-day Hay Ground Road in Bridgehampton, just north of the Montauk Highway. They rented a house and 15 acres of farmland on which Louis grew potatoes and feed corn. Five more children were born in this house: Jessie, Alice, Bertha, as well as Helen and Benjamin, who both died before they reached two years of age. The family spoke Polish at home but with the exception of Anna, all eventually became fluent in English.

In 1914 Louis rented the farm where Bill and Joan Zaluski live today, on the crest of Deerfield Road. Three years later he was able to buy an impressive Victorian house farther north on Deerfield, surrounded by 90 acres of farmland and 10 acres of woodland. What

Louis was able to accomplish was astounding. In just 20 years, through skillful husbandry and considerable sacrifice, he ascended from immigrant laborer to the owner of a splendid home and a prosperous farm.

Alice and Bertha, nicknamed by their father "Sam" and "Bow," are now in their nineties. They savor memories of a happy childhood in the big Victorian on Deerfield Road. They remember their father walked "as straight as a ramrod" and that he used to say "A man is not a man without a beard." He played the violin, mostly lovely Polish folk songs or rousing Polkas, and though he didn't read music he could listen to a tune once and play it back. He became a popular performer for local weddings and parties. Every Sunday, Alice and Bertha recall, their father would hitch up the horse-drawn surrey and drive the entire family to Southampton for services at the Catholic church. After church, aunts and uncles, cousins and kin would gather at the big Victorian house for games, food and wonderful times.

Deerfield Road in the 1920's was an unpaved dirt road and had only two other houses. The Zaluskis had a horse pasture, a milk cow, pear trees, a 20-tree apple orchard and red and white grape vines. They also had a smokehouse for pork and a root cellar where they stored the turnips, cabbage, carrots and potatoes that they grew in a meticulously maintained vegetable garden.

If Louis' hard work bootstrapped the family to financial independence and home ownership, Anna's steadfast labors kept the big family fed, happy, and together. Alice and Bertha remember their mother Anna always at home making delicious meals for the family. They would rush home from school to the big farm kitchen, redolent with the smell of crepes or warm buns with butter. There was always something warm to eat on the back of the stove. Anna made bread three times a week and ice cream when the weather was warm. She was an excellent seamstress and made all the family's clothes.

The big house, built in the early 1900's, had an indoor bathroom and hot water heat provided through radiators by a coal-fired furnace. For the first ten years the Zaluskis lived in the house, they used kerosene lamps. When electric poles were raised on Deerfield Road in 1924, Louis had the house wired and installed fixtures in every room. The first night they had electricity the Zaluskis turned on every light in the house and gathered outside in the yard to see it. Bertha remembers "it looked just like a big hotel." The house had a big wrap-around porch, which was covered with roses all summer long. Bertha learned to roller skate on this porch, circling the house time and again while her brother Stanley yelled at her for loosening the floorboards. The family all helped keep the house and grounds in a pristine state. Their father would collect rocks which they white-washed and carefully placed, as Alice says, "just so, along the driveway."

Under their parents' direction, the Zaluski clan did all kinds of chores around the home and farm. The privet hedges that surrounded the house were neatly hand-clipped at waist height, to enable a passing neighbor to be seen and greeted and to keep the panoramic view of farmland, visible from all the rooms in the house. After the fall harvest, farmers and their families would cut firewood from the forest. Incidentally, this allowed more sunlight to reach the forest floor, encouraging the growth of brambles. In the spring and summer, children scrambled home from the woods with pails full of berries for pies and jams.

In 1925, at age 60, Louis died of cancer. Anna, with sons Stanley, then 28, and William, then 24, assumed the responsibility for operating the farm and caring for the six girls. As Polish tradition dictated, Stanley, the oldest son, managed the operation. This same year both Stanley and William married. Stanley married Dorris Backas, a school teacher from a one-horse town thirty miles from the Canadian border, and moved his bride into the Victorian with his mother and sisters. William married Harriet Scholtz, the daughter of a local farmer, and they settled into a simple frame rental house on Montauk Highway in Water Mill. William and Harriet's first child, Barbara, nicknamed "Bobby," was born in 1925. Three years later, the current Zaluski patriarch, Bill, nicknamed "The Colonel," followed.

Stanley and William worked the farm together. They bought their first truck in 1930. Until then, they had relied solely on the strength of horses to pull their plows and wagons. The daily operation of the farm continued to be a family endeavor. The girls drove the truck all day in the fields during the harvest while potato sacks were filled and loaded on, and helped hand-cut potatoes for seed.

In 1931 Anna Zaluski purchased the 40-acre farm that she and Louis had rented from 1914 to 1917, just south of her Victorian home on Deerfield Road. With that, the present-day dimensions of the Zaluski farm were established, at a total of 140 acres. Since Stanley had the Victorian, Anna gave the newly acquired farmhouse to William and his burgeoning family. The two-story house had running water but no bathroom. Anna next divided the two farms, giving each son half the acreage of the two contiguous farms combined. As is the custom of many farm families, land is bequeathed to sons, money and possessions to daughters. The assumption is that daughters will marry men with land. By this time Stella, Helen and Martha had married local farmers, while Alice and Bertha had married local plumbers.

Stanley was gradually becoming disenchanted with the financial responsibility and uncertainty of farming. In 1939 he left Long Island for Niagara, New York, to work in the wartime aircraft industry. He returned to Long Island after the war but never to the family farm. For many years after, he worked as a foreman of the A&P potato-loading facility in Water Mill, until his death in a plane crash during a snowstorm in East Hampton, in the winter of 1956. His brother Bill, though, loved the farming life. So did little Bill – "the colonel". He was "tied to his father's back pocket from the time he could walk," as many farmer's sons are described. Young Bill disliked school and longed each year for summer, when he'd join his father in the fields, and for the 15-day-long harvest break that local schools gave farm-family children in autumn. In September of 1943, the year he turned fifteen, Bill asked his father which 15 days he should take off from school as his harvest break. His father suggested the first half of October. On October, 15, Bill's mother called the principal to say her son would only be returning to school to retrieve his books from study hall. He did just that, and turned 16 the following day. He says that although he's had a lot of happy days in his life, this day, which was the end of school for him, was the happiest. The next morning he began helping his father full time growing potatoes. He says he had little time for anything else, with the exception of occasionally hunting, crabbing or playing poker with friends.

Bill was 19 when his grandmother died at home of pneumonia and an enlarged heart. Three years later, he married Joan Bennett Webber of Amagansett, a stunning beauty and award-winning poet. She and Bill renovated the barn behind William and Harriett's farmhouse and moved in. Joan managed to fit well into the arduous routine of running the farm. A typical day began at 3:30 a.m. When breakfast was finished and the dishes cleared and cleaned, both Joan and her mother-in-law Harriet might help drive a truck for the day. Or they might drive to Riverhead to pick up fertilizer. There was coffee and rolls to prepare for a mid-morning break for the men in the fields, and a ten-minute-long "pit-stop" lunch to prepare so the men could keep working. They continued until dark: "can till you can't," as Bill puts it. The worst year Bill remembers was 1985. The drought that year was so bad that from 100 acres of potatoes, the harvest fit in one picker's apron. That year it cost the farmers more to grow a crop than they earned. "Every spring there's usually one or two auctions of farms, but that year there were a lot."

Eventually Bill's father bought his first potato harvester, and put an end to the desultory work of manual harvesting. He and Bill carried on together, each with the invaluable help of their wives, until William died of heart failure in 1987. The main house was renovated, and Bill and Joan moved in with Harriet, having lived in the renovated barn for 39 years and raised four boys there. Joan cared for Harriet until she, too, died of heart failure in 1992. Joan's own mother, who was ailing, moved in as well until the end of her life. The Zaluskis, like many farm families in the East End, took as a given the responsibility of caring for their elders.

Of Bill and Joan's four sons, only the oldest, Billy, has taken to farming. Billy's first job on the farm was carrying lunch to the men in the fields. At four or five years old, he remembers "throwing empty potato bags off the back of a tractor and men picking up potatoes." With the exception of Sunday, every day was spent working on the farm. Once the school year began, he would spend seven hours in the classroom and immediately come home to help on the farm. During the harvest he was permitted to leave in the middle of the school day. Billy always knew he would end up farming. Like most farmers, he doesn't like to work inside or be hemmed in by crowds. Like his father, he loves to plow and can't wait for spring after being cooped up all winter. He says the first half hour of the day, as the sun rises, is his favorite time of day. Out in the fields, alone, is where he finds his greatest peace.

Billy recognizes his father's love of farming and farm life. "Even after his heart surgery, he was right back in the fields," he says of his father. "The Doctor told Dad that he couldn't plow anymore, but he was on a tractor the next day." When I asked him what it was like working with his father he replied, "He's very fussy about how a farm's run and you can argue with him if you want, but in the end his methods work."

Billy now runs the family farm stand – a job more aggravating than his father's. From February to September he must overcome the countless challenges of growing a variety of food crops as well as contend with the problems inherent in running a retail operation, including grouchy customers. He has six greenhouses behind his home on Water Mill Towd Road, adjacent to his parents' home on Deerfield, just a quick truck ride along a headland that bisects the farm. To meet the demands of the farm stand he grows about forty acres of vegetables, flowers and sweet corn and thirty more acres of potatoes. Once the farm stand opens, usually on Mother's Day, there are no days off, even if it rains. From the beginning of August to Labor Day, he and his crew work fifteen-hour days. "You have to keep on your toes all season," Billy says. "There's no such thing as down time." By the end of the season he's usually made a good income for the year, but the workload is crushing.

The future of the Zaluski Farm is unclear even though much of the land has been protected. Joan and Bill worked closely with the Peconic Land Trust to provide their sons with the opportunity to continue farming. Most of the development rights on the farm were sold to Southampton Town to create liquidity, thereby reducing the inheritance tax burden of the farm itself. They created a small number of building lots for their family members as well. They have also formed a family limited partnership and each year the boys are gifted a percentage interest in the land. Ultimately, the farm will transfer out of Joan and Bill's taxable estate. After Bill and Joan are gone, the sons can sell the farmland in one piece, but it can only be used for agricultural purposes. Billy has two daughters from previous marriages but neither intends to carry on the family tradition of farming. Perhaps one of his brother's sons will decide that farming is in his blood and continue the dedication begun by Louis at the turn of the last century and passed down to William, Bill and now Billy.

Beezer

Bill "The Colonel" or "Beezer" Zaluski, 1949, at a Southampton beach.

SPRING

Highland Terrace from Ocean Road, Bridgehampton.

Preparation for spring begins the previous fall when next year's crops are planned and seeds and plant plugs are ordered. By February, every piece of equipment has been thoroughly checked and repaired, so that when the weather is right, it is ready to go. Lastly, the machines will be scrubbed and buffed "like debutantes," as Marilee Foster describes it, in preparation for their coming-out parties in the fields.

Farmers in early spring are edgy like horses at a starting gate, ready to start plowing and planting but careful not to start too soon or too late. Potatoes are the first crop planted, and the trickiest to gauge. An April freeze can ruin seed in the ground, but starting late as a safeguard means a late harvest for each successive crop through the season, and stressful months of catch-up. Lee Foster says she no longer worries because "these guys have a sixth sense about when to plant."

Spring's unpredictable weather conditions dictate the day's activities. Very wet and cool conditions make planting a frustrating stop-and-go process with downpours halting tractors mid-field. Everyone's gotten a tractor, tool or even a boot, stuck in the mud at least once. As John Halsey puts it, "When the weather's good, you go and get as much done as you can before it rains again." For an early crop, Adam Halsey plants sweet corn under long sheets of protective plastic laid by machine over the planting beds, but cold or cloudy weather can undermine the most carefully considered plans.

The air is full of promise and excitement. Perennial taunting of rival farms begins, with false reports of who was the first to plow, or start their sweet corn, and later, who finished planting potatoes. New ideas to improve yields are tried in an endless process of invention and improvisation. That struggle is a centuries-old tradition and the foundation of a successful farm.

Greenhouses at every farm are fired up now, becoming tropically warm. They turn the cold outside to luxuriant spring inside, first with an explosion of flowers, then with lush green waves of tiny, vulnerable vegetables, a shocking contrast to the gray pall of late-winter days. Apple trees are filled with flower buds, waiting for enough warmth to open and be pollinated by the wind or expectant bees, who prefer to perform their vital job on warm, sunny days.

Plowing might begin at the end of March, if weather permits. As the blades of the plow break the soil's winter seal, chocolate brown soil spills out in luxuriant arcs. Redolent with a cool green promise, the first spring plowing is an evocative and fulfilling time for every farmer. Once a field is tilled, the next morning a mist forms from warmth of the newly exposed earth making contact with the cooler air. It evaporates with the rising sun, withdrawing across a field in phantom forms.

Dean Foster and Jigger Howe planting potatoes, near Sagg Pond, Sagaponack.

Jimmy Backer and Junior, Foster Farm, Sagg Main Street, Sagaponack.

Ted McCoy and Cliff Foster in the farm shop, Foster Farm.

Amy Halsey's greenhouse, White Cap Farm, Mecox Road, Water Mill.

Foster Farm shop door.

Foster Farm shop yard.

Tom Conklin spreading lime on a Corwith field,
Seven Ponds Road, Water Mill.

Michael Sachtleben watching over potato seed cutting, Zaluski Farm,
Deerfield Road, Water Mill.

Charles Johnson and Wallace Brinson planting Forsythia, Corwith Tree Farm, Water Mill Towd Road, Water Mill.

Mark Corwith loading Forsythia, Corwith Tree Farm.

Jigger Howe checks potato seed planting, Kinkade Farm,
Parsonage Lane, Sagaponack.

Dean Foster and Jigger Howe loading potato planter with potato seed and fertilizer, at Sagg Pond.

Bill Zaluski plowing on Deerfield Road.

Ted McCoy and Jimmy Baker ordering for spring, Foster Farm.

1941 Minneapolis Moline.

Dean Foster discing, Highland Terrace.

Jimmy Comfort in tractor cab-pulling the potato planter. Cliff Foster plows the field ahead of him, Sagg Main Street, Sagaponack.

Dicky and Mark Corwith fertilizing at the tree farm.

Corwith Farm, Head of the Pond Road, Water Mill.   Cliff Foster's 1960's Farmall, Foster Farm.

Adam Halsey discing, Halsey Farm, Deerfield Road, Water Mill.

Tom and Adam Halsey receiving flats of flower plugs, Halsey Farm.

Yolanda Lean and Victor Rojas prepare flower flats, Halsey Farm.

Amy Halsey in her greenhouse, Whitecap Farm.

Tom Halsey in the greenhouse, Halsey Farm.

Corwith Hereford cows, Corwith Farm,
Head of Pond Road, Water Mill.

John Halsey in the apple orchard, Whitecap Farm.

Plants under plastic, Zaluski Farm.   Zaluski Farm looking southeast, Water Mill.

Dean Foster and "Jigger" Howe check potato seed and fertilizer placement, Sagaponack.

Dean Foster repairing equipment in the farm shop.

Billy Zaluski loading potato seed, Deerfield Road, Water Mill.

Marilee and Dean Foster conferring, Parsonage Lane, Sagaponack.

Adam Halsey plowing, Halsey Farm.　　　　Zaluski fertilizer and potato seed, Deerfield Road, Water Mill.

Dean Foster, Jimmy Comfort and Jigger Howe check the calibration of the potato planter, Sagg Main Street, Sagaponack.

Cliff Foster plows up to the sand dunes,
Daniel's Lane, Sagaponack.

Potato Planter, Town Lane, Amagansett.   Dean Foster discing, Town Lane.

Shedrick barn, Highland Terrace, Sagaponack.

Lee, Marilee and Dean Foster with Jigger Howe and Jimmy Comfort stopping for
a picnic lunch, Kinkade Farm, Parsonage Lane, Sagaponack.

Bill and Joan Zaluski's home, Zaluski Farm,
Deerfield Road, Water Mill.

Retreating mist at Kinkade farm, Parsonage Lane.

Charles Johnson stacking Forsythia, Corwith Tree Farm.

Bill Zaluski crabbing on Mecox Bay.

Adam Halsey on a tractor with roll-over plow, Halsey Farm.   Tom Halsey, Halsey Farm.

John Halsey planting apple trees, Whitecap Farm.

Paul Corwith, Corwith Farm.

Greenhouse, Halsey Farm.

Zaluski Farm, Water Mill.

Dicky Corwith, Corwith Farm.

Whitecap Farm house.

Long Island Antique Power Assoc. Spring Plow Day,
Highland Terrace, Bridgehampton.

Zaluski Farm looking east, Water Mill.

Watching the Spring Plow Day,
Highland Terrace, Bridgehampton.

Billy and Bill Zaluski planting sweet corn, Zaluski Farm.

Jenn Halsey's peach trees, Milk Pail, Montauk Highway, Water Mill.

Apple blossoms at Whitecap Farm.

Dot Halsey, Halsey Farm.

Meredith White and Christy Grzybowski in a Zaluski Greenhouse.

Foster wildflower field, Hedges Lane, Sagaponack.   Dicky Corwith's house, Head of Pond Road, Water Mill.

Foster potato blossoms, Sagg Main Street, Sagaponack.

Apple blossoms, Whitecap Farm.

SUMMER

Everyone's hopes and dreams seem to rise and bloom with the warmth of the summer sun. On the East End, the crowds and traffic are at their peak. The beaches are blanketed with a patchwork of colorful umbrellas and the towels of people renewing themselves at the ocean's edge, as they have been since the 1850's. Just over the dunes are acres of fragrant tilled earth studded with tiny white stars: potato blossoms. In fields beside them, a dramatically different story is unfolding: the dark green plumage of corn.

As Dean Foster cultivates a potato field on Daniels Lane at 6:00 a.m., the sound of his tractor mixes with the roar of the surf. He listens to the ocean with a keen ear: if the waves hold, he may finish his long work day on his surf board. Moving large pieces of equipment in summer is done at dawn, along with much of the picking of vegetables, flowers and fruits for the day. Sweet corn may be picked a few times over the course of a day to ensure optimum freshness. Most people won't ever rise early enough to see the enormous effort made each day to keep the fields and farm stands at their best.

By July, the fields are yielding a banquet of food as well as a summer-long banquet for the senses. A field of rye in the July sun smells like fresh-baked cinnamon buns. Oat fields are molten gold, shimmering against the unbroken blue of summer sky. Farms stands are packed with overflowing baskets of piquant vegetables, fruits and flowers, luxuriously fresh after being picked that morning. In a few weeks, apple and peach trees will be pruned to allow sunlight to reach branches full of ripening fruit. The days are long, especially for farms with stands that require constant care to keep a profitable balance between ever-ripening produce and customer demand.

A dry summer can test the most resolute farmer. When there's no rain, and no access to nearby water to irrigate a field, every day burns slowly by. Most beachgoers don't even notice a drought until it's become severe. They marvel at the steady procession of sunny days, oblivious to the damage taking place all around them, and the sleepless nights that farmers spend as they move irrigation pipes from field to field. Too much rain can be just as devastating — sometimes worse than drought, because nothing can be done about it. But when summer is good for farmers, the fields intermittently moist and dry as crops reach toward the sun, the world sings a verdant opera to the enormous benefit of us all.

Rye and field corn, Narrow Lane, Water Mill.   Tom Halsey fertilizing, Halsey Farm.

Sayre Field, Butter Lane, Bridgehampton.

Zaluski Farm, Deerfield Road, Water Mill.

South of Daniel's Lane, Sagaponack.

Fosters irrigating potatoes, Hedges Lane, Sagaponack.

Jimmy Comfort plows under rye, Fairfield Pond Road, Sagaponack.

Marilee Foster on her Allis-chalmers model G, Foster Farm.

Flowers at Halsey Farm.

Bill Zaluski on his 1947 Red Farmall, Zaluski Farm.　　　　Tomato plants under plastic, Halsey Farm.

Foster field corn, northwest of Sagg Pond, Sagaponack.

Zaluski Farm Stand, Upper Seven Ponds Road, Water Mill.   Adam Halsey planting in plastic, Halsey Farm.

Foster Farm Stand, Sagg Main Street, Sagaponack.

Foster Farm Stand.

Anastasia Rojas polishing tomatoes, Halsey Farm.

Cliff Foster and Button, Foster farm shop.

Cliff Foster, Foster farm shop.

Michael Sachtleben and Christy Grzybowski picking string beans, Zaluski Farm.

Amy, Jenn, Evelyn and John Halsey at lunch, Whitecap Farm.

Dean Foster and Ted McCoy move irrigation on a potato field,
Hedges Lane, Sagaponack.

Billy Zaluski at the Zaluski Farm Stand, Seven Ponds Road, Water Mill.

Melon picking at Halsey Farm.

Corwith Potato blossoms, Head of Pond Road, Water Mill.

Marilee Foster and field corn, Montauk Highway, Bridgehampton.

Foster Farm Stand, Sagg Main Street, Sagaponack.

Ted McCoy and Jigger Howe move irrigation pipe,
Daniel's Lane, Sagaponack.

John Halsey checks his bee hives, Whitecap Farm.

Comfort Farm, Lumber Lane, Bridgehampton.

Marilee Foster on afternoon break, Foster farm shop.

Bill Zaluski's Aunts, "Bow" Zaluski Petty and "Sam" Zaluski Bruzdoski,
Water Mill.

Christy Grzybowski, Zaluski Farm.

Amy Halsey's greenhouse, Whitecap Farm.

Jadwiga Kucmierowscy picking vegetables at Halsey Farm.

Jigger Howe moving irrigation pipe, Daniel's Lane, Sagaponack.

Irrigating sweet corn, Halsey Farm.

Dot Halsey and Nicky, Halsey Farm.   End of Labor Day, Halsey Farm.

Stuart Foster, Upper Seven Ponds, Water Mill.

Adam Halsey and Yolanda Leon planting leeks, Halsey Farm.

Lee Foster bikes to the Sagaponack Post Office.

Beth Halsey and Erica Cerami attend the Halsey Farm Stand.

Meredith White picking sun flowers, Zaluski Farm Stand.   Adam and Tom Halsey, Halsey Farm.

Zaluski Homestead, Deerfield Road, Water Mill.

Rich Corwith bailing hay, Blank Lane, Water Mill.

Corwith Rye, Head of the Pond Road, Water Mill.

Dan Carroll picking sweet corn, Zaluski Farm.

Billy Zaluski picking sweet corn, Zaluski Farm.

Stuart Foster combining hay, Head of Pond Road, Water Mill.

Dicky Corwith baling hay with son Rich Corwith,
Blank Lane, Water Mill.

Corwith hay bales.

Foster field corn at Comfort Farm, Lumber Lane, Bridgehampton.

Picking apples, Whitecap Farm.

Ace Red Delicious apples, Whitecap Farm.   Jenn Halsey loading baskets of peaches, Milk Pail, Water Mill.

FALL

The harvesting of potatoes heralds fall. Huge machines move slowly through the rows of dried potato vines like prehistoric herbivores. A century ago, the work was done by hand — many hands. In 1920, the first mechanical potato digger, a horse-drawn invention, somewhat eased the back-breaking labor. A generation later came tractor-pulled harvesters, and with them an end to the manual work. Today potatoes are harvested with thrilling efficiency. The tubers are dug out mechanically, separated from their vines, funneled into trucks that drive alongside the latest harvesting machines, then poured by bin loaders into barns for storage.

Field corn, used for animal feed, is harvested next, as soon as it's dry in the field. Field corn was a minor crop on Long Island until mechanized combines arrived in about 1950, because it had to be picked by hand, stored in corn cribs until needed, then shelled, one ear at a time, by a shelling machine. Today corn combines separate the cobs from the stalks, then the kernels from the cobs, sending a golden stream into a waiting truck. Once harvested, the kernels are carefully dried in huge grain dryers to reduce the moisture content — thereby preventing mold — then stored in silos. Corn will be shipped and sold, usually to a mill in Eastport, throughout the winter and into the spring.

By September, apples are being picked, along with the late vegetables; pumpkins, squash, kale and cauliflower. Cut from the fields, their vibrant colors adorn farm stands that stay open through fall.

Cover crops of oats or rye must be planted after each field has been harvested to help keep the vulnerable topsoil from blowing away. Oats are sown by October, before the weather is too cold. When the blades are six or seven inches high, they rustle in the wind like emerald-green rapids. Rye is hardier and can be planted later. It also has deeper roots than oats and these help loosen compacted soil. For the East End farmers, planting a cover crop is followed by discussions about how to keep the Canada geese — ubiquitous fall visitors now — from eating it. A sizable flock can pluck an eight-acre field clean, overnight. By then, it may be too late in the season to plant another. To thwart the geese, farmers plant plastic streamers, set off firecrackers, or even arrange metal cutouts of leaping sprites throughout their fields like an Indonesian puppet show.

When the potato trucks are unloaded, a first grading takes place. Men stand by the conveyor belt that moves potatoes from a truck onto mountainous piles inside the storage barn, and pluck out clearly rotten or damaged ones. When the potatoes are sold, they're graded again. Now large ones – the "A's" — are washed and put in 50-, 20-, 10-, or 5-pound bags for market. The smaller "B"s are washed or "floomed" and sold in bulk for canning.

Farms with apple orchards grade their harvest as well. First the apples are washed and sized. Apples that are 2 3/4" and above are graded "fancy." Smaller apples are used for cider. Next, the fancy apples are hand sorted for defects, then carefully packed in wood crates and stacked in refrigerated barns for storage.

If you visit a farm in winter where potatoes are being graded, you might at first think it's deserted. Then you hear a muffled rumbling and clanking sound that comes usually from the biggest barn. Inside, the barn is aglow with the golden-yellow light thrown off by thousands of potatoes rolling down brightly-lit conveyor belts that snake up and down, this way and that. Slowly, you make out workers moving through the dusty light. The air is so full of soil you can taste it.

The average potato-yield per acre on an East End farm is about 400 bags, with each bag large enough to hold 100 pounds. If a farmer grows 300 acres of potatoes, that gives him an overall yield of 120,000 bags. By a conservative estimate, each of those "hundred-weight" bags holds 100 potatoes. If you do the math you'll come up with 12 million potatoes that have to be graded, washed and bagged. Prices have ranged from a low of $.88 per hundred weight in 1940 to a high of $8.85 in 1980. It's amazing to realize how many people a single family farm can feed.

Everyone tries to be finished harvesting by Thanksgiving Day but regardless, the day is enjoyed by all with pride and relief.

Jimmy Comfort scooping potatoes from a storage cellar for grading, Foster Farm.

Jimmy Comfort in "Nadine" prepping soil for cover crop, Sagaponack.

Ted McCoy checking the depth of the potato harvester, Sagaponack.

Grading potatoes, Corwith Farm.

Fosters harvesting potatoes, Sagaponack.

Harry "Slim" Henderson unloading potatoes, Foster Farm.

Dean and Marilee Foster clear vines from the potato harvester, Sagaponack.

Jigger Howe flooming the "B's", Foster Farm.

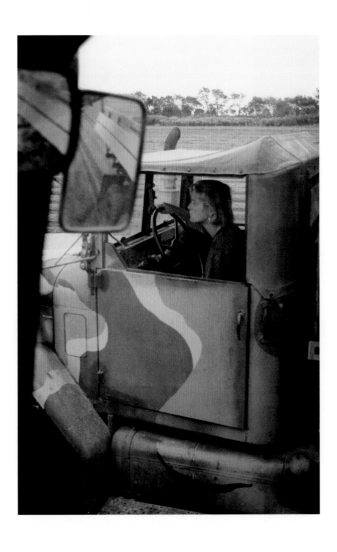

Marilee Foster driving the potato truck, Sagaponack.

Purple Cauliflower, Sagg Road, Sagaponack.

Highland Terrace ready for a Foster cover crop, Bridgehampton.

Marilee Foster harvesting cauliflower, Sagg Road, Sagaponack.

Foster Farm Halloween Pumpkins, Sagg Main Street, Sagaponack.

Alex Cooper and Francis Lester grading potatoes at Foster Farm.

Dean Foster driving the potato harvester, Sagaponack.

Old apple tree, Whitecap Farm.

Jenn Halsey opening the honey comb cells, Whitecap Farm.

John Halsey at the family's "U-Pick", Horse Mill Lane, Whitecap Farm.

Washing apples, Whitecap Farm.

Mark Corwith unloading potatoes, Corwith Farm.

Peach baskets, Corwith Red Barn, Water Mill.   Corwiths harvesting potatoes, David White's Lane, Water Mill.

Evelyn Halsey weighing and bagging apples, Milk Pail,
Montauk Highway, Water Mill.

Apple trees at Whitecap Farm.

Meredith White and Dan Carroll take down the Zaluski
Farm Stand, Seven Ponds Road.

Billy Zaluski securing new plastic on a hoop house, Zaluski Farm.

Bill Zaluski with Scallop, Zaluski Farm.

Bill Zaluski grading on the potato harvester, Zaluski Farm.

1872 well house, Halsey Farm.

Pumpkins and gourds, Halsey Farm greenhouse.

Lemuel Halsey's house, Halsey Farm.

Phragmites, Sagg Pond.

Zaluski potato field ready to harvest, Deerfield Road, Water Mill.

Zaluski potato harvester, Zaluski Farm.

Maple Trees, Sagaponack.

Aerial view of Whitecap Farm, Mecox Road, Water Mill.

Foster field corn at Comfort Farm, Lumber Lane, Bridgehampton.

Foster field corn at Comfort Farm.

Fosters harvesting field corn, Montauk Highway, Bridgehampton.

Cliff Foster.

Dean Foster and Ted McCoy untangle the corn combine,
Montauk Highway, Bridgehampton.

Fosters harvesting field corn, Comfort Farm, Bridgehampton.

Corn auger and silo, Foster Farm.

Corwiths unloading field corn, Water Mill.

Corwiths unloading field corn, Water Mill.

Cliff Foster combining field corn, Comfort Farm,
Lumber Lane, Bridgehampton.

Harvested field corn, Lumber Lane, Bridgehampton.   Field corn ready to harvest, Bridgehampton.

Field corn ready to harvest, Montauk Highway, Bridgehampton.

Harvesting field corn, Highland Terrace, Bridgehampton.

Tom and Dot Halsey, Thanksgiving Dinner, Halsey Farm.

Marilee, Lee and Cliff Foster with Guy Flemming at
Thanksgiving, Foster Farm.

Dean and Cliff Foster after dinner.

WINTER

What do farmers do in the winter? Many assume they go south like an exotic avian species, disappearing when the weather cools. This is of course not true. They remain here, feeling cooped-up inside their homes like the rest of us, still busy with the constant demands of a farm. Almost every farmer I've spoken to has said that farm work is never done; not for the day, the season or the year. Any time that a farmer takes off is just stolen from some task waiting to be done. Even in the deepest winter when they need time off the most - after nine months of rising before dawn and retiring after dusk - farmers must carefully plan vacation or travel because each member of the family is indispensable.

Even at play, however, farmers keep an ear cocked for local emergencies. Many are members of the local volunteer fire and rescue services. They have emergency pager radios that squawk twenty-four hours, seven days a week. One recent winter evening, I went over to the Fosters' for dinner. Several times during the meal the table suddenly fell silent to listen to the tones and numeric codes coming from Cliff's pager on the kitchen counter as it monitored the various emergency calls, in the event he or his son Dean were needed.

Money management is the backbone of a farm, as it is with any business, so at least one person spends hours bent over receipts and records, scratching away with a finely sharpened pencil. Farmers mastermind new techniques for sowing or harvesting. They weigh the merits of introducing new produce, or new ways of marketing the produce they already grow.

While the bookkeepers of the family are doing the ledgers, others might be out in their machine shops, repairing and maintaining the fleet of machines needed to run a farm. Nothing is more frustrating than a tractor, combine or harvester breaking down in a field, and aside from bad weather, nothing slows down the planting or harvesting schedule as much. They also continually transform their equipment to be more efficient, as farmers have done for centuries. Meanwhile, potatoes still need to be graded and bagged as they go to market, and at apple farms, cider is still being made.

Outside, the cold winds of winter storms will have turned rye into a tangled blond mass and oat fields look like camel hair blankets laid across the landscape. Apple trees are pruned in winter when they are dormant. This renewal pruning adjusts the shape of the tree, removes older, less productive wood and stimulates the growth of new branches, called spurs, which produce the highest-quality fruit.

One of the few diversions that can inexorably lure farm families from their work in the winter is ice on any body of water. It takes a brave soul to shimmy out on the first ice - called "bendigo" ice because it "bends as you go" - in order to break a hole in it and measure the thickness to see if there's enough to hold an iceboat. It's usually one of the statesmen, such as Bud Topping or John or Tom Halsey. They check the fresh water ponds first; Mill Pond, Poxabogue and Long Pond, and then the brackish Mecox Bay, which freezes last. Then, when the weather's right and the wind's up they're on the ice gliding as gracefully as water striders at speeds up to 60 miles per hour. Age is no deterrent to enjoying this sport; young and old "hike up" on two blades as they twist and play with the gusts of wind. One recent winter the ice was so thick that in a fit of joy Dean Foster swooped down in his airplane, touched his tires on the ice of Mecox Bay and swooped up again. The family members take turns for each other on the farm so they can go off to enjoy one of their favorite sports, and one of the oldest, before the fickle ice yields to inconstant weather and inevitable spring.

By February farms are beginning to warm up their greenhouses and receive their first cuttings and seedlings. The tempo picks up frenetically even with snow on the ground and seemingly endless days of freezing rain. One would think these families would dread the onset of spring and the whole cycle beginning again but, as early as the first of March they are champing at the bit to be in the fields again.

John Halsey, Whitecap Farm.

Nicky Halsey, Halsey Farm.

Amy Halsey's greenhouse, Whitecap Farm.

Marilee Foster's sculptures to frighten geese, Sagg Main Street.   Corwith field of Oats, Head of the Pond Road, Water Mill.

Frank Ruppel, expert tractor mechanic, Halsey Lane, Bridgehampton.　　　　　　Foster potato cellar, Foster Farm.

Foster potato harvester at rest, Montauk Highway, Bridgehampton.

Corwith red barn, Seven Ponds Road, Water Mill.

South of Daniel's Lane, Sagaponack.

Claes Cassel pruning apple trees, Whitecap Farm.   South of Daniel's Lane, Sagaponack.

Discer, Foster corn field, Bridgehampton.   Highland Terrace oat field, Bridgehampton.

Winter field looking northwest to David White's Lane, Southampton.

Phragmites at the end of Horse Mill Lane, Water Mill. Hendrickson house, Lumber Lane, Bridgehampton.

Sydnee on the porch at Hendrickson House.

Mark and Kelly Corwith fix breakfast, Head of Pond Road, Water Mill.

Dot Halsey sets her table for Christmas dinner, Halsey Farm.

Christina, Robin and Rich Corwith, Corwith Farm, Water Mill.   After Christmas Dinner, Halsey Farm.

Adam and Dot Halsey, Halsey Farm.

Jocelyn Halsey Armusewicz, Halsey Farm.

Kelly, Jill and Samantha Corwith, Head of Pond Road, Water Mill.

Claes Cassel making apple sauce, Whitecap Farm.

Corn stalks at Halsey Farm.

Zaluski homestead, Deerfield Road, Water Mill.

Phragmites at Sagg Bridge, Sagaponack.

Corwith Farm.

Corwith Farm.

Foster field across from Poxabogue, Bridgehampton.   Zaluski Farm looking east.

1954 Farmall, Foster Farm.

Cliff and Lee Foster's home, Foster Farm.

Tom and Dot Halsey's home, Halsey Farm.

Potato cellar, Foster Farm.

Ice boating, Mecox Bay, Water Mill.   Tom and John Halseys' ice boat, 'Penguin,' Mecox Bay.

Bud Topping, Mecox Bay.

John Halsey in 'Penguin,' Mecox Bay.

Kinkade Farm, Parsonage Lane, Sagaponack.

Corwith Farm, Water Mill.   Daniel's Lane, Sagaponack.

Greenhouses, Halsey Farm.

Zaluski Farm, looking north.   Whitecap Farm entrance.

Dean Foster in the farm shop.   Jigger Howe in the Foster farm shop.

Ted McCoy welding, Foster farm shop.   Tom Halsey, Halsey Farm.

Oat field, Wainscott.

Halsey Farm house.

Sunset, Bridgehampton.

Sunset, East Hampton.

Sunset, Montauk Highway, Bridgehampton.

Aerial view of South Fork.

ACKNOWLEDGMENTS

I still have not come up with a satisfactory explanation for why the Halseys, Fosters, Corwiths and Zaluskis, allowed me to photograph them over the course of a year. Whatever their reasons, I'm so grateful to them for their kindness and friendship, and for their confidence in this project.

"True East" was a dream of mine that grew with the help of a few very special people who follow and fulfill their own dreams as a matter of course. If David McHugh hadn't offered to loan me the cameras I used, this project would never have begun. If Peter Hill hadn't loaned me his great knowledge of photography and keen sense of color, it wouldn't have turned out as well as it did. John v.H. Halsey of the Peconic Land Trust took an enthusiastic interest from the start, introducing me to more kindred souls who could help: Ngaere Macray and David Seeler and Paul Brennan. Ralph Carpentier and Betsey Pinover Schiff helped me edit thousands of photographs to chose the ones in these pages. Claudia and John Thomas and Scott Chronis extended their excellent counsel and business savvy throughout. Thanks also to Phil and Susan Dusenberry, Mr. and Mrs. John Erwin, Jen and Jim Pike, Mr. and Mrs. Otis Pearsall, John White and Sann and John Van Deventer for their generous support.

I found crucial historical records for "True East's" farming families and their colonial forebears at the Southampton Historical Museum. Thanks so much to museum directors Richard and Rosanne Barrons, and David Goddard, for their encouragement and help.

I'm not sure a writer can have enough editors. Harvey Loomis took a pass at my first draft, as did Heyward Isham. Fred McCormack helped, too. Thanks, most profoundly, to Michael Shnayerson. All four skillfully and painlessly refined my text.

When the pictures and text of this book were nearly assembled, Peter Jones and Nicholas Callaway gave me invaluable advice on how to get it published. They led me to Sue Medlicott and Steven Mosier of Working Dog Press, who produced "True East" with great style and professionalism.

Thanks above all to the hard-working, not-for-profit visionaries of the Peconic Land Trust, who helped sponsor "True East" as a celebration of the precious, working farms they're trying so hard to save on Long Island's East End: its Board, staff and President , John v.H. Halsey. Many thanks also to Dan Shedrick, Pingree and Don Louchheim, for their llth-hour support.

SUGGESTED READING

Adams, James Truslow. *Memorials of Old Bridgehampton*. New York: Ira J. Friedman, Inc., 1969.

Bridenbaugh, Carl. *Vexed and Troubled Englishmen: 1590-1642*. New York: Oxford University Press, 1968.

Bryson, Bill. *A Short History of Nearly Everything*. New York: Broadway Books, 2003.

Chaskey, Scott. *This Common Ground*. New York: Viking Penguin Group, 2005.

Fischer, David Hackett. *Albion's Seed: Four British Folkways in America*. New York: Oxford University Press, 1989.

Foster, Marilee. *Dirt Under my Nails*. Bridgehampton, New York: Bridge Works Publishing Company, 2002

Fraser, Antonia. *The Lives of the Kings & Queens of England*. Berkeley: University of California Press, 1998

Gabriel, Ralph Henry. *The Evolution of Long Island*. New York: Ira J. Friedman, Inc., 1960.

Matthiessen, Peter. *Wildlife in America*. New York: Viking Penguin Inc., 1987.

Pope, Charles Henry. *The Pioneers of Massachusetts*. Maryland: Genealogical Publishing Co., 1998

Willison, George Findlay. *Saint and Strangers: the story of the 'Mayflower' and the Plymouth Colony*. London: Heineman, 1966.

Villani, Robert. *Long Island: A Natural History*. New York: Harry N. Abrams, Inc., 1997.

Zawadzki, Hubert and Lukowski, Jerzy. *A Concise History of Poland*. Cambridge: Cambridge University Press, 2001.